W9-BFW-629

YELLOWSTONE
NATIONAL PARK

BY FRANCES NAGLE

Gareth Stevens
PUBLISHING

Please visit our website, www.garethstevens.com. For a free color catalog of all our high-quality books, call toll free 1-800-542-2595 or fax 1-877-542-2596.

Library of Congress Cataloging-in-Publication Data

Nagle, Frances.
  Yellowstone National Park / Frances Nagle.
     pages cm. — (Road trip: National Parks)
  Includes index.
  ISBN 978-1-4824-1691-6 (pbk.)
  ISBN 978-1-4824-1692-3 (6 pack)
  ISBN 978-1-4824-1690-9 (library binding)
  1. Yosemite National Park (Calif.)—Juvenile literature. I. Title.
  F722.N36 2014
  979.4'47—dc23

                                         2014031946

First Edition

Published in 2016 by
Gareth Stevens Publishing
111 East 14th Street, Suite 349
New York, NY 10003

Copyright © 2016 Gareth Stevens Publishing

Designer: Andrea Davison-Bartolotta
Editor: Kristen Rajczak

Photo credits: Cover, p. 1 (right) Kenneth Keifer/Shutterstock.com; cover, p. 1 (left) Flashon Studio/Shutterstock.com; cover, back cover, interior (background texture) Marilyn Volan/Shutterstock.com; pp. 4, 6, 8, 10, 12, 14, 16, 18, 20 (blue sign) Vitezslav Valka/Shutterstock.com; pp. 4, 6, 8, 10, 12, 14, 16, 18, 20, 21 (road) Renata Novackova/Shutterstock.com; p. 4 Rainier Lesniewski/Shutterstock.com; p. 5 Jason Patrick Ross/Shutterstock.com; p. 6 W.H. Jackson/The New York Historical Society/Getty Images; p. 7 MPI/Getty Images; p. 9 (both) NPS.gov/Wikimedia Commons; pp. 10, 21 (map) Globe Turner, LLC/Getty Images; p. 10 silky/Shutterstock.com; p. 11 Tom Murphy/National Geographic/Getty Images; p. 12 gary718/Shutterstock.com; p. 13 Jeff Banke/Shutterstock.com; p. 14 Krzysztof Wiktor/Shutterstock.com; p. 15 tjwvandongen/Shutterstock.com; p. 16 schrojo/Shutterstock.com; p. 17 (main) Frederic Labaune/Moment/Getty Images; p. 17 (inset) Russell Burden/Stockbyte/Getty Images; p. 19 Jochen Lambrechts/Shutterstock.com; p. 20 Edward Fielding/Shutterstock.com; p. 21 (notebook) 89studio/Shutterstock.com.

Printed in the United States of America

CPSIA compliance information: Batch #CS16GS: For further information contact Gareth Stevens, New York, New York at 1-800-542-2595.

Contents

Words in the glossary appear in **bold** type the first time they are used in the text.

Why Visit Yellowstone?

Yellowstone National Park is the oldest national park in the United States. It's also one of the largest. Yellowstone has been a popular place for a road trip since cars were first allowed in the park in 1915. Covering parts of northwestern Wyoming, southwestern Montana, and eastern Idaho, Yellowstone has millions of visitors every year.

Today, people head to Yellowstone National Park to hike through the beautiful mountains and forests found in the park. They hope to see **unique** wildlife and, of course, check out the amazing water features!

Yellowstone National Park

MONTANA

IDAHO

WYOMING

CHAYENNE

UTAH

COLORADO

All About Yellowstone National Park

where found: parts of Wyoming, Montana, and Idaho

year established: 1872

size: 3,472 square miles (8,992 sq km)

number of visitors yearly: about 3 million

common wildlife: bison, black bears, coyotes, woodpeckers, elk

common plant life: lodgepole pines, Douglas firs, wildflowers such as phlox and Indian paintbrushes

major attractions: Old Faithful, Upper and Lower Falls of the Yellowstone, Specimen Ridge

Yellowstone National Park is the fourth most visited national park in the United States.

Pit Stop

Three major mountain ranges are found in Yellowstone National Park: the Gallatin Range, the Absaroka Range, and the Teton Range.

5

People's Place

It's believed that people have lived in the Yellowstone area for about 13,000 to 14,000 years. Around the year 1400, one group of Shoshone Indians began living there. It wasn't until 1807 that white explorers came to Yellowstone.

Soon, fur trappers and those interested in the **topography** and special water features made their way to Yellowstone. The first map of the area was made in 1836, and by the 1870s, studies about the land were being done.

Mammoth Hot Springs, 1871

Pit Stop

The first Yellowstone traveler, John Colter, had been exploring the new western territory of the United States with a group before leaving them and finding the Yellowstone area.

Images of Yellowstone like this one drew more people to it during the mid-1800s.

More Protection Needed

In the 1860s, people began asking the US government to **protect** the most beautiful natural areas of the country. They worried people's activities would harm the **environment**. Yellowstone was the first of these areas to become a national park in 1872.

It wasn't enough, however. Hunters were killing too many animals, and visitors weren't taking care of park property. In 1886, the park was put under the care of the US Army. Soldiers patrolled the park for **poachers** and built new buildings.

Pit Stop

The National Park Service was created in 1916. It took over Yellowstone National Park soon after.

Fort Yellowstone building from 1909

In 1910, 324 soldiers were stationed in Yellowstone National Park. They lived in groups of buildings called Fort Yellowstone, which visitors can still visit today.

Eruption!

How the land looks in Yellowstone National Park today is partly a result of shifting **tectonic plates**. About 2 million years ago, a **volcano** that had been forming for a long time blew up. It **erupted** again about 700,000 years later, and two more times after that. These events left behind a caldera, or a huge, bowl-shaped landform.

Today, the Yellowstone volcano is still active! Scientists watch the activity around it carefully, but they don't think it will erupt again anytime soon.

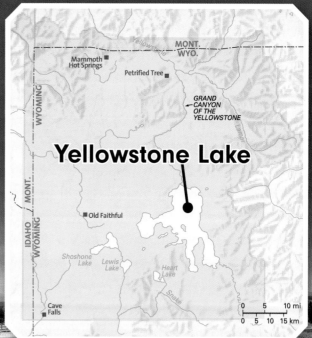

When visiting Yellowstone National Park, visitors can fish on Yellowstone Lake as well as take a boat tour of the park.

Pit Stop

Post

Much of the Yellowstone Caldera is full of water and called Yellowstone Lake.

Another Grand Canyon

The Grand Canyon of the Yellowstone formed between 10,000 and 14,000 years ago. The Yellowstone River wore away rock to create a canyon that's 20 miles (32 km) long.

The Yellowstone River created another cool site to visit—the Upper and Lower Falls of the Yellowstone. At 308 feet (94 m) high, the Lower Falls are taller than Niagara Falls by about 140 feet (43 m)! Adventurous visitors can hike up a short, steep trail to the top of the falls.

Tower Fall

Pit Stop

When the park was established in 1872, an artist painted another waterfall in Yellowstone National Park called Tower Fall. That's just one of the many other waterfalls in the park!

The Lower Falls in the Grand Canyon of the Yellowstone is one of the most photographed places in the park.

Old Faithful

Perhaps the most well-known site at Yellowstone National Park is Old Faithful. This **geyser** is found in the Upper Geyser **Basin** located west of the center of the park. It "faithfully" erupts about every 90 minutes, earning its name by staying on time!

There are about 300 other geysers in Yellowstone. In fact, visitors can find about 10,000 **hydrothermal** features throughout the park, including hot springs you can bathe in! All these occur due to **magma** heating water underground.

Pit Stop

About 60 percent of all the world's geysers are found in Yellowstone National Park.

Within 1 square mile (2.6 sq km), there are 150 geysers in Yellowstone, including Old Faithful.

15

Forest Home

Though Yellowstone is a hot spot for hydrothermal features, about 80 percent of the park is covered by forest. Many of these are lodgepole pine forests.

The forests provide a great home for animals such as foxes, elk, and mule deer. Songbirds and woodpeckers are the most common birds found in the park, though about 300 kinds live there for part of the year. Along the lakes and streams of the park, beavers can be found, and many kinds of trout swim in these waters.

Pit Stop

Post

Viewing wildlife at Yellowstone National Park can be great fun! Hayden Valley is a good place to see grizzly bears, bison, wolves, and coyotes.

Up to 5,000 bison live in Yellowstone National Park. It's the only place in the United States where bison have lived continuously for thousands of years.

Specimen Ridge

Yellowstone National Park has the greatest number of petrified trees in the world. "Petrified" means "turned to stone." Trees become petrified over a long period of time as **minerals** replace the wood.

Many petrified trees are found at Specimen Ridge. However, one stands alone in the northeast part of the park. Simply called the "Petrified Tree," this tree was once a redwood in a forest of other redwoods. It was petrified following Yellowstone's volcanic eruptions, which killed the other trees around it.

Pit Stop

Many other plant fossils can be found at Specimen Ridge, too. Fossils are the hardened marks or remains of ancient plants and animals.

Petrified trees are also a kind of fossil. The great number of them at Yellowstone National Park can teach scientists what Earth was like long ago.

Adventure Awaits!

Because there are so many cool natural features throughout Yellowstone National Park, visitors often camp there for several days to see it all. Hikers can try out more than 1,000 miles (1,609 km) of trails, including a popular hike to the top of Mount Washburn more than 10,000 feet (3,048 m) up!

From Old Faithful to herds of bison, Yellowstone National Park offers amazing sights anyone would enjoy. It truly shouldn't be missed on your next road trip!

Pit Stop

Don't miss the 45th Parallel Bridge. When standing on it, visitors are halfway between the equator and the North Pole!

Grand Prismatic Spring

Yellowstone National Park

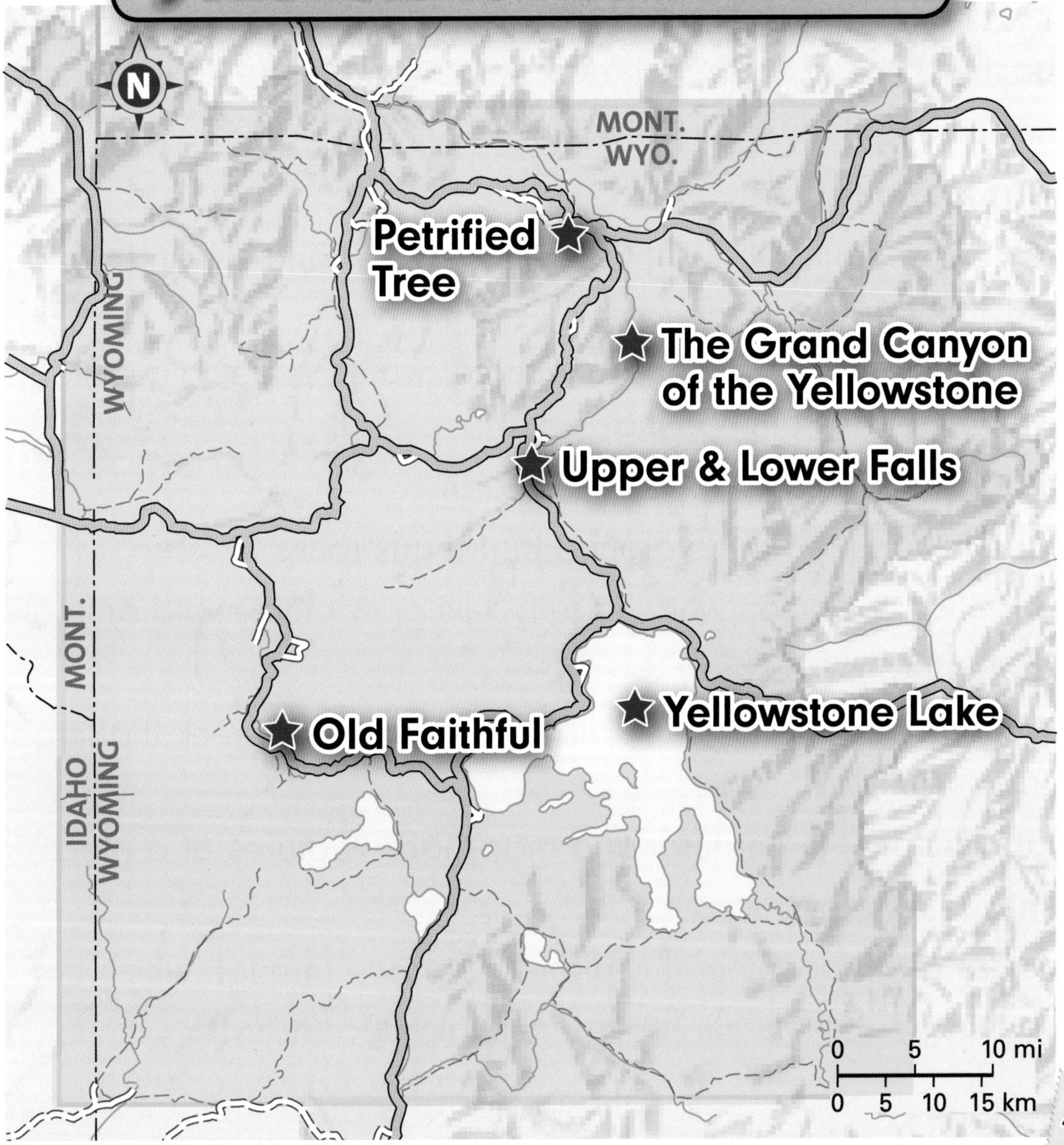

N

MONT.
WYO.

WYOMING

IDAHO | MONT.
WYOMING

★ Petrified Tree

★ The Grand Canyon of the Yellowstone

★ Upper & Lower Falls

★ Old Faithful

★ Yellowstone Lake

0   5   10 mi
0 5 10 15 km

Glossary

basin: a dip in Earth's surface, somewhat shaped like a bowl

environment: the natural world in which a plant or animal lives

erupt: to burst forth

geyser: a spring that shoots heated water and steam from a crack in Earth

hydrothermal: having to do with hot water, especially mixed with minerals from cooling

magma: hot, liquid rock inside Earth

mineral: matter in the ground that forms rocks

poacher: a person who illegally kills or captures wild animals

protect: to keep safe

tectonic plate: one of the moveable masses of rock that create Earth's surface

topography: the natural and man-made features of a place

unique: one of a kind

volcano: an opening in a planet's surface through which hot, liquid rock sometimes flows

For More Information

Books

Frisch, Nate. *Yellowstone National Park.* Mankato, MN: Creative Education, 2014.

Graf, Mike. *Yellowstone National Park: Eye of the Grizzly.* Guilford, CT: FalconGuides, 2012.

Websites

For Kids—Yellowstone National Park
www.nps.gov/yell/forkids/index.htm
Find information on activities for kids visiting Yellowstone and websites to visit to learn more about it.

Fun Facts
www.yellowstonepark-trip.com/fun-facts-about-yellowstone-park.php
Learn lots of cool facts about Yellowstone National Park.

Index